The Glory Ride

Road Racing

Written by   Jay Denan

Troll Associates

Printed in the United States.of America. Troll Associates, Mahwah, N.J.
Library of Congress Catalog Card Number: 79-52179
ISBN 0-89375-254-1   (0-89375-255-X soft cover ed.)

Photo credits: Dan Rubin, BMW, British Leyland

Tires screech on the turns.

Powerful engines whine, as sleek sports cars thunder along twisting roads. They roar over hills and screech around hairpin turns. Here is excitement. Here is danger. Here is the ultimate test for driver and machine. This is road racing—the glory ride.

Down the straightaway at LeMans, France.

Road racing began in France in the late nineteenth century. It quickly spread to Italy, which became known as the "home" of European road racing. Road races have been held in the United States since the early twentieth century. Today's races, however, are much different from those of yesterday.

Rounding a turn and heading for home.

In the early years of road racing, each car held two people—a driver and a mechanic. Later on, each car carried only one person. Sometimes a team of drivers would take turns driving a car. Each new driver would take over for a certain part of the race—like in a relay.

A high-powered sports car streaks past the crowd.

In 1897, a road race was held around Lake Maggiore (Mah-JO-ray) in Italy. It boasted six cars, four motorcycles, and two tricycles. None of the motorcycles finished. But a tricycle came in third. The winner's speed was 22 kilometers an hour (13.5 miles an hour). Today, road-racing machines often reach speeds of well over 320 kilometers an hour (200 miles an hour).

Modern road circuits have curves and hills.

Soon after the race at Lake Maggiore, another famous road event began. Called the *Targa Florio,* it was held in Sicily, a large island off the southern Italian coast. The roads were narrow, dirt-packed, and twisting. The race snaked around the island, then over hills and through olive groves. Modern road races still include hills, turns, and winding stretches.

There's no time for a nap in today's fast-paced road races.

Some strange things happened in the early years of the *Targa Florio.* A driver once ran out of gas and borrowed a bicycle to finish. The judges said it was against the rules. Another year, a British driver won. His time would have been faster if he had not decided, in the middle of the race, to lie down for an hour's nap. Luckily, he had a two-hour lead!

Today, flag marshals signal road conditions.

Road racing soon became popular in North and South America. The famous races in Argentina were called *Grandes Premios*. They ran up and down the country. They were often more than 8,000 kilometers (5,000 miles) long. Most modern road races are shorter, but excitement is still the one word that best describes what they offer.

Another well-known race was the *Mexican Road Race*, or *Pan-American Road Race*. It was run on the part of the Pan-American Highway that winds through Mexico, from Guatemala to the United States. The biggest problem was getting gas and repairs. Gassing up during a modern road race is no problem. But high speeds create other problems.

Down a hill on the Atlanta road course.

Unpaved roads and broken rocks made up the last 144 kilometers (90 miles) of the Mexican Road Race. One year, the race leader blew *seven* tires over that hazardous stretch! And lost the race. Good tires are still important today, even though most road races are run on paved roads.

Racing through the night.

In 1909, one race was from New York to Seattle, Washington. Henry Ford entered two Model T's in the race. One was the winner. The car averaged a speedy 12.4 kilometers an hour (7.75 miles an hour)! It covered more than 6,400 kilometers (4,000 miles) in a little over three weeks. Modern road races don't take that long. But some continue right through the night.

Fighting to keep awake!

One of the most famous road races was the *Mille Miglia* (MILL-uh MEEL-yuh), which means "thousand miles." It was held in Italy, and was 1,600 kilometers (1,000 miles) in length. It was a grueling course with mountain curves, city streets, and stretches of highway. Wind and rain, sun and darkness. And danger—of leaking fuel, of blown tires, of driving fatigue. The same dangers threaten drivers today.

A one-eyed monster roars around a slippery turn.

In a road race, the winner is the one who finishes the race in the shortest time. But there is more involved than speed. Will the car hold up under the strain of constant pressure driving? Will the road become slippery from rain? Will a tire blow? Will the fuel last? Will there be an accident?

Denise McLuggage races a Ferrari through the rain.

Road racing has always appealed to drivers from many different countries. In Porsches and Lotuses, in Ferraris and Triumphs, they come to test their cars and themselves. Each driver wants to prove that he or she is the best. From the days of the earliest *Mille Miglia* to the present day, both men and women have competed for honors in the exciting sport of road racing.

Battling for position on the turns.

When road races were held on public streets, the right-of-way was blocked off to traffic for the race. Barriers at certain points kept spectators from coming onto the course. Bales of straw were piled at dangerous spots. In today's crowded world-on-wheels, it is difficult to close public roads even for a short time.

Out of control!

Too many accidents and too many fatalities led to the last of the famous road races of the past. The Mexican Road Race lasted only from 1950 to 1954. The last *Mille Miglia* was held in 1957. The *Targa Florio* ended in 1973. Now most road races are held on special racing circuits. Safety has become a very important factor—for spectators, as well as drivers.

A safe vantage point.

When a road race is held on a special road course, public roads don't have to be closed. Admission can be charged to spectators, who can watch the action from the safety of the grandstand, or from cliffs or hills overlooking the circuit.

Checking the cars out.

In the United States, road races are held at Laguna Seca in California, at Limerock in Connecticut, at Watkins Glen in upstate New York, and at other road courses. Before each race, the car is thoroughly checked out by expert mechanics on the racing team. The engine must be tuned perfectly. Nothing is left to chance.

Buckling up before the race.

Safety equipment is essential. Drivers wear fireproof racing suits. Seat belts and shoulder harnesses help keep the driver in the car in case of a crash. A sturdy roll bar helps protect the driver, if the car should spin out of control and start to roll over.

Action at LeMans.

In Europe, famous road-racing circuits include LeMans in France, and the Nurburgring in Germany. The Nurburgring is 22.8 kilometers (14.2 miles) long, with rolling hills and 36 sharp turns. LeMans is about 13.4 kilometers (8.4 miles) in length, with long straightaways and winding curves.

Running for the cars.

In the past, many road races began with the LeMans start. A flag signaled the start of the race. Then the drivers ran to their cars, jumped in, started their engines, and raced off as fast as they could. Sometimes, it was confusing. Often, it was dangerous.

The scramble for position.

The LeMans start is no longer used in the United States. It is still sometimes used in European road races, but the drivers are already sitting in their cars. Their safety belts are fastened before the starting flag drops. Then, at the signal, their engines come to life, and they roar out onto the course.

In position before a rolling start.

Most road races today begin with a rolling start. The cars are lined up in their positions before the race begins. The cars with the best positions are the ones that have made the best time in the qualifying runs. The drivers in the front positions have a double advantage. They have the fastest cars. And they are already at the head of the pack.

The pace car leads the parade lap.

In a rolling start, the powerful racing machines follow a pace car around the circuit for a parade lap. They must keep in their assigned positions. Suddenly the pace car speeds up and pulls off the road into the pit area, and the race is on! The sound of roaring engines shatters the air.

Everything must be perfect.

Hundreds of sports car races are held each year. Many of the drivers are amateurs, who want to get in on the thrill and excitement of road racing. In the Sports Car Road Racing Championship, cars are divided into several classes, depending on the size of their engines. The less powerful cars don't have to race against the more powerful ones.

Getting ready for a Can-Am race.

The Canadian American Challenge Cup is a series of road races for skilled professionals. They drive only special racing cars, called Can-Am cars. These low-slung machines run on the same kind of fuel as regular sports cars, but they can reach speeds of over 320 kilometers an hour (200 miles an hour).

Modern Grand Prix and "formula" cars are wedge-shaped.

Grand Prix racing is the most glamorous form of road racing today. Grand Prix cars have no fenders. The cockpit barely has room enough for the driver. Most of these cars are made in Europe, where Grand Prix racing was born in 1906. The first Grand Prix was held at LeMans.

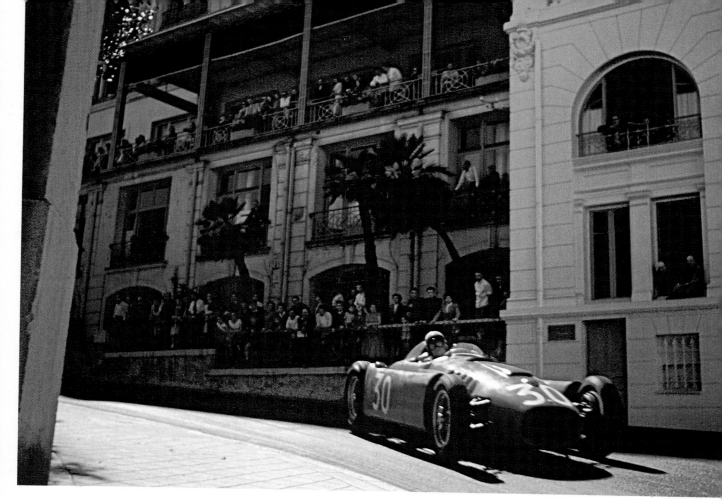
High speeds in the streets of Monte Carlo, Monaco.

The United States holds two Grand Prix races. One is held on the road course at Watkins Glen, N.Y. The other is held in Long Beach, California. Grand Prix races are also held in 16 other countries throughout the world. The most exciting Grand Prix is held in the tiny European country of Monaco. It is one of the few road races that still take place on city streets.

Practicing for the Monaco Grand Prix.

The through-the-streets road race—where daredevil drivers grimly push their cars to the limit as they sweep around tight curves and scream down country roads—is becoming a thing of the past. If there were a way to make these races safer for drivers and spectators, through-the-streets road races might become widely accepted once again.

Looking under the hood of a dream machine.

There are many who say that road racing is the most exciting of all motor racing. Once you are bitten by the road-race bug, they say you will never recover. Instead, you will dream of that perfect car—the car that will stand up to anything the most challenging road course can throw at it.

The glory ride!

You will think of the cheering crowds as you thunder past, and of the cars you have already passed on the road. You will think of the hills and the curves that lie on the course ahead, and of the way the powerful machine responds to your every command. This is what it's all about. This is road racing—the glory ride.